APPLES

APPLES

southwater

This edition published by Southwater

Distributed in the UK by
The Manning Partnership
251-253 London Road East
Batheaston, Bath BA1 7RL, UK
tel. (0044) 01225 852 727
fax. (0044) 01225 852 852

Distributed in the USA by
Ottenheimer Publishing
5 Park Center Court
Suite 300
Owing Mills MD 2117-5001, USA
tel. (001) 410 902 9100
fax. (001) 410 902 7210

Distributed in Australia by
Unit 1, 360 Norton Street
Leichhardt
New South Wales 2040, Australia
tel. (0061) 2 9560 7888
fax. (0061) 2 9560 7488

Distributed in New Zealand by
Five Mile Press NZ
Unit 3/46a Taharoto Road, PO Box 33-1071
Takapuna, Auckland 9, New Zealand
tel. (0064) 9 486 1925
fax. (0064) 9 486 1454

Southwater is an imprint of
Anness Publishing Limited
© 1996, 2000 Anness Publishing Limited

1 3 5 7 9 10 8 6 4 2

Publisher: Joanna Lorenz
Senior Cookery Editor: Linda Fraser
Cookery Editor: Anne Hildyard
Designer: Lisa Tai
Illustrations: Anna Koska

Photographers: Karl Adamson, Edward Allwright, Steve Baxter, Michelle Garrett,
Nelson Hargreaves, Amanda Heywood, Tim Hill and Don Last
Recipes: Carla Capalbo, Carole Clements, Norma MacMillan,
Laura Washburn and Elizabeth Wolf-Cohen
Food for photography: Frances Cleary, Carole Handslip, Wendy Lee, Jane Stevenson,
and Elizabeth Wolf-Cohen
Stylists: Hilary Guy, Sarah Maxwell, Blake Minton, Kirsty Rawlings and Fiona Tillet

Typeset by MC Typeset Ltd, Rochester, Kent
Previously published as *Apples: A Book of Recipes*
Printed and bound in Singapore

For all recipes, quantities are given in both metric and imperial measures and,
where appropriate, measures are also given in standard cups and spoons.
Follow one set, but not a mixture, because they are not interchangeable.

Contents

$\mathcal{I}$NTRODUCTION

We've all been there: about to crunch into a huge, shiny red apple and positively salivating at the prospect. One bite, however, and instead of crisp, juicy flesh and sweet, aromatic taste, it is woolly-textured and devoid of any flavour at all. As far as apples are concerned, size is not important.

In order to select apples which have good, old-fashioned flavour, you should use your nose, not your eyes. When choosing apples – whether it is from a high street greengrocer or the supermarket shelves – apply the smell test. A good apple will have a pleasing, lightly perfumed aroma. The smell and taste of a decent apple can vary from a rich, fragrant Cox's Orange Pippin to a scented Worcester Pearmain. An inferior one – such as many of the imported Golden and Red Delicious – all too often has a powdery texture and virtually no aroma. The apple is a fruit which thrives best in a temperate climate and there are thousands to choose from. Recently, growers have been encouraged to plant old-fashioned varieties with a definite emphasis on flavour, so there is now hope that home-grown apples can resume their role as our most splendid and highly-prized national fruit.

All through history, apples have played a starring role. From Eve's downfall in the Garden of Eden to present-day Hallowe'en toffee apples, they have been associated with providence, tradition and with the fundamentals of life.

One of the most versatile of fruits, they can combine with an astonishing array of flavours; sweet and savoury.

This book is divided into five chapters. The recipes begin with salads, soups and dips in the first chapter, the second includes lovely ideas such as Somerset Pork with Apples and Guinea Fowl with Cider and Apples. The next chapter has five variations on apple pie: with strawberries, upside-down Tarte Tatin, lattice-topped Dutch Apple Tart, meringue-peaked tart and the classic apple pie. The hot puddings which follow will have you drooling: choose from Eve's Pudding, Apple and Blackberry Nut Crumble or the wonderfully innovative Apple Couscous Pudding. Finally, cold desserts feature Apple and Hazelnut Shortcake flavoured with fresh mint, and a frozen fruit terrine.

Use apples in abundance – to add a sweet yet tangy flavour to your meat, fish and vegetables; and to add fragrance to myriad sweet puddings and cakes. This delightful little book will be sure to inspire you with new ideas about how to use our favourite and most versatile of fruits, apples.

Sue Lawrence

$\mathscr{A}$PPLE $\mathscr{V}$ARIETIES

GOLDEN DELICIOUS

Widely available, this variety has yellow skin and pale flesh. Crisp and sweet, it is good eaten raw.

WORCESTER PEARMAIN (also known as Worcester)
This small apple is sweet and is best eaten raw.

FUJI

This apple has greenish-yellow skin with a rosy blush and is sweet and juicy. Excellent in salads.

GRANNY SMITH

This is a sharp and firm eating apple that is ideal for use in both sweet and savoury dishes.

COX'S ORANGE PIPPIN (commonly known as Cox)
A fine English dessert apple with yellow, juicy flesh.

ALKMENE

A recent variety, this sweet eating apple is yellow-skinned with a red blush and has soft-textured flesh.

ROYAL GALA

This red-skinned apple has firm and sweet white flesh. It is excellent for both eating and cooking.

RED DELICIOUS

Well known for its deep red colour, it has a tough skin and slightly mushy flesh, and is best eaten raw.

BRAEBURN

A very sweet, juicy and crisp eating apple with a red skin, this can be eaten raw, in salads and sauces.

BRAMLEY

This cooking apple is large, green and acid in flavour. It is ideal for sauces with savoury dishes.

FISHER'S FORTUNE

A crisp dessert apple that is new to the market.

CHARLES ROSS

A juicy new variety that is good for eating raw.

Golden Delicious

Cox's Orange Pippin

Worcester Pearmain

Fuji

Granny Smith

Alkmene

Royal Gala

Red Delicious

Braeburn

Bramley

Charles Ross

Fisher's Fortune

$\mathscr{P}$REPARED $\mathscr{A}$PPLES

Apples seem to have been with us forever and are to be found in all kinds of recipes. Staple fruits that grow well in many parts of the world, apples can be bought fresh, bottled, canned and dried. In any guise their tangy sweetness enhances and complements main ingredients. They feature in a large variety of both sweet and savoury recipes, from apple amber to apple salad, from chutney to casseroles and from stuffings to sauces.

DRIED APPLE RINGS AND CHUNKS

To reconstitute, cover in boiling water and leave for an hour or two then simmer until tender.

They are ideal for use in winter fruit salads, breakfast compotes, muesli, mousses, purées, sauces, cold and hot puddings, and fruit cakes.

BOTTLED CHUNKY APPLE

This can be eaten as a simple dessert with yogurt or cream or used in cooking to make quick sauces, purées, fools, cakes or hot puddings.

BRAMLEY APPLE SAUCE

Serve this ready-made apple sauce with goose, game, chicken or meat dishes, particularly pork. For a quick dessert, stir into Greek-style yogurt.

CANNED APPLE SLICES

These are useful for making pies, tarts or apple cake and are perfect for making quick hot or cold puddings.

APPLE SLICES

Apple slices can be used as a garnish for savoury dishes and add an attractive decoration to fresh fruit desserts, mousses or fools.

ROYAL GALA WEDGES

When cut into wedges, this is a delicious apple to eat as a snack or served as part of a fruit platter.

GRANNY SMITH HALF AND QUARTER

These apples are good for cooking because of their firm flesh and piquant flavour. Cut into halves or quarters, and use in apple tarts and cakes.

RED DELICIOUS GARNISH

To make the garnish, cut an apple in half, make a series of V-shaped cuts in the apple, then fan out.

FISHER'S FORTUNE HALF AND QUARTERS

Cut into halves or quarters, it can be served as a quick snack or dessert with slices of cheese.

Apple slices

Bottled chunky apple

Royal Gala wedges

Granny Smith
half and quarter

Canned apple slices

Red Delicious garnish

Fisher's Fortune
half and
quarters

Dried apple rings

Dried apple chunks

Bramley apple sauce

Basic Techniques

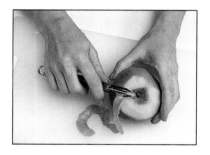 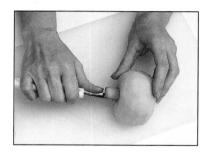 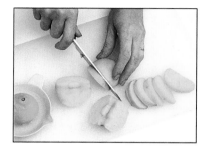

Use a small sharp knife or peeler to remove the skin from the apple. Starting at the top, peel around the apple, turning it as you go, taking off as little as possible.

To remove the core when the apple is to be cooked whole, use an apple corer. Push the corer firmly through the centre of the apple and pull it out with the core in it. (If the apple is to be sliced or chopped, you can cut out the core with a knife after quartering it.)

Before slicing or chopping, cut each apple in quarters. Take each quarter and cut into even slices. If the apple is not used immediately, brush the slices with lemon juice to prevent them from discolouring. When preparing apples for apple sauce, simply slice or chop them roughly after removing the core.

Freezer Tips

Cooked apples are excellent candidates for the freezer because they thaw well without significant loss of flavour or texture. They must be prepared for freezing in purée form for sauces, or as ready-made pie filling.

After making the sauce or pie filling, cool completely then spoon into either waxed cartons or polythene bags. Seal the containers well before freezing.

● *Choosing and buying apples*: unlike many other fruits, apples have no off season in the supermarket – they are now available all year round. The varieties you can buy at different times will vary, however. Apples are in abundance in many countries from summer to late winter. In general, when cooking choose firm and sharp varieties that will give a good flavour. The dark red-skinned or soft, sweet apples are best eaten raw.

● *Peeled apples*: if not using them straight away, brush them or dip them in lemon juice to prevent the apples from turning brown.

● *Poaching apples*: this method is used when the apple is required to keep its shape in the cooking. Simmer the slices or whole peeled apples gently in syrup in a saucepan for two or three minutes, then turn off the heat and finish the cooking in the residual heat with the lid on.

● *Baking apples*: when baking whole cooking apples, a good way to prevent the skins from bursting in the oven, is to score a shallow line in the skin around the circumference of each apple using a sharp knife.

● *Storage of apples*: apples can be stored in many ways, depending on their ultimate usage. If you grow your own or can buy in bulk, eating apples can be stored whole for up to 6 months by wrapping in paper and packing in boxes in a cool, dry place. Remember that they must not be bruised or damaged before storing, and always check them regularly to remove any that have rotted or the rest will spoil.

● *Preserving apples*: apples can be successfully frozen (see Freezer Tips, left) and also make good jams, jellies, chutneys, pickles, and even wine. They are suitable for bottling but since they are more usually preserved by other methods, this is not common. Another method of home preservation is to dry apple rings then store them in jars. Dried apple rings and slices can also be bought from supermarkets and health food shops and soaked before making pie fillings, sauces or simply dropped into casseroles. They make a delicious snack and can also be finely chopped and added to home-made muesli.

Starters and Light Meals

Fresh flavourful apples sharpen up parsnip soup and mackerel dip, add a tart tang to fig and date salad, and give a pleasing crunchiness to potato cakes and pittas.

SMOKED MACKEREL AND APPLE DIP

Serve this quick fishy dip with tasty curried bread dippers.

Serves 6–8

*350g/12oz smoked mackerel, skinned
  and boned*

*1 soft eating apple, peeled, cored and
  cut into chunks*

150ml/¼ pint/²⁄₃ cup fromage frais

pinch of paprika or curry powder

salt and ground black pepper

apple slices, to garnish

For the curried dippers

4 slices white bread, crusts removed

25g/1oz/2 tbsp butter, softened

5ml/1 tsp curry paste

COOK'S TIP

*Instead of using plain sliced
bread, try other breads for the
dippers – Italian ciabatta, rye
bread, or pitta breads would
be excellent.*

Place the smoked mackerel in a food processor or blender with the apple, fromage frais and seasonings. Blend for about 2 minutes or until the mixture is smooth. Check the seasoning, then transfer to a small serving dish and chill. Preheat the oven to 200°C/400°F/Gas 6. To make the curried dippers, place the bread on a baking sheet. Blend the butter and curry paste thoroughly, then spread over the bread.

Cook the bread in the oven for about 10 minutes, or until crisp and golden. Cut into fingers and serve, while still warm, with the mackerel dip, garnished with the apple slices.

PARSNIP AND APPLE SOUP

A hearty, warming soup that's excellent served on a cold winter's day.

Serves 8–10

50g/2oz/4 tbsp unsalted butter

2 large onions, sliced

1 garlic clove, chopped

2 large parsnips, scrubbed and cubed

2 cooking apples (about 450g/1lb),
  peeled, cored and cubed

10ml/2 tsp medium curry powder

1.5 litres/2½ pints/6¼ cups
  chicken stock

300ml/½ pint/1¼ cups single cream

salt and ground black pepper

For the topping

25g/1oz/2 tbsp unsalted butter

115g/4oz/1 cup pecans, chopped

150ml/¼ pint/⅔ cup crème fraîche or
  soured cream

Heat the butter in a large pan and sauté the onions and garlic over moderate heat until the onions are translucent. Stir in the parsnips and apples and sauté for a further 3 minutes, stirring occasionally. Add the curry powder and stir to mix. Cook for 1 minute more. Pour on the stock, bring to the boil, cover the pan and simmer for 20 minutes. Remove from the heat and cool slightly. Pour into a food processor or blender and process until smooth. Return the soup to the pan. Stir in the cream and seasoning and heat gently.

To make the topping, heat the butter in a pan and sauté the pecans over moderate heat for 5 minutes. Serve the soup in bowls topped with the crème fraîche or soured cream and sprinkled with the sautéed pecans.

CHICKEN AND APPLE PITTAS

Pittas are great for a teenage party – just supply the ingredients and let the party-goers assemble their own.

Serves 4

¼ red cabbage

1 small red onion, finely sliced

2 radishes, finely sliced

1 red eating apple, peeled, cored
   and grated

15ml/1 tbsp lemon juice

45ml/3 tbsp low-fat fromage frais

1 cooked chicken breast (about 175g/
   6oz), skinned

4 large or 8 small pittas

salt and ground black pepper

chopped fresh parsley, to garnish

COOK'S TIP

*If the filled pittas need to be
made more than an hour in
advance, line the pitta breads
with crisp lettuce leaves before
adding the filling. Cover and
chill until required.*

Remove the tough central spine from the cabbage leaves, then finely shred the leaves using a large sharp knife. Place the shredded cabbage in a large bowl and stir in the onion, radishes, apple and lemon juice.

Stir the fromage frais into the shredded cabbage mixture and season well. Thinly slice the cooked chicken breast and stir into the shredded cabbage mixture until thoroughly coated in the fromage frais.

Preheat the grill. Place the pittas on the grill pan and toast until warmed. Split them along one edge with a round-ended knife. Spoon the filling into the pittas. Serve immediately garnished with the parsley.

FIG, APPLE AND DATE SALAD

Sweet Mediterranean figs and dates combine especially well with crisp eating apples.

Serves 4

6 large eating apples

juice of 1/2 lemon

175g/6oz fresh dates

25g/1oz white marzipan

5ml/1 tsp orange flower water

60ml/4 tbsp natural yogurt

4 fresh green or purple figs

4 toasted almonds, to garnish

COOK'S TIP

When buying fresh dates, avoid any that look shrivelled. They should be plump and shiny, yellow-red to golden brown and with smooth skins.

Core the apples and slice thinly with a sharp knife. Leave the skins on. Cut into fine matchsticks. Place in a bowl and moisten with lemon juice.

Remove the stones from the dates and cut the flesh into fine strips, then combine with the apple slices in the bowl.

In a separate bowl, soften the marzipan with orange flower water and combine with the yogurt. Mix together well until smooth.

Divide the apples and dates among the centre of four plates. Remove the stem from each of the figs and divide the fruit into quarters without cutting right through the base. Squeeze the base with the thumb and forefinger of each hand to open up the fruit. Place a fig in the centre of each salad, spoon in the yogurt filling and serve garnished with a toasted almond.

POTATO CAKES WITH APPLE

These potato cakes resemble latkes, *a Central European dish. Work quickly, as the potato darkens rapidly.*

Makes about 16

15g/¹/₂oz/1 tbsp butter

1–2 eating apples, unpeeled, cored and diced

5ml/1 tsp lemon juice

10ml/2 tsp sugar

pinch of cinnamon

50ml/2fl oz/¹/₄ cup thick soured cream

flat leaf parsley, to garnish

For the potato cakes

¹/₂ small onion, very finely chopped or grated

2 baking potatoes

oil for frying

salt and ground black pepper

Heat the butter in a frying pan over moderate heat. Add the diced apple and toss to coat. Stir in the lemon juice, sugar and cinnamon. Cook for 2–3 minutes, stirring, until the apples are just tender and beginning to colour. Turn into a bowl.

To make the potato cakes, place the grated onion into a bowl. Grate the potatoes on to a clean dish towel and squeeze the potato dry. Add the potatoes to the onion and season. Heat 1cm/¹/₂in oil in a large heavy-based frying pan until hot. Drop tablespoonfuls of the potato mixture into the oil in batches. Flatten slightly and cook for 5–6 minutes. Drain on kitchen paper. Serve each potato cake topped with 15ml/1 tbsp caramelized apple and a little soured cream, garnished with parsley.

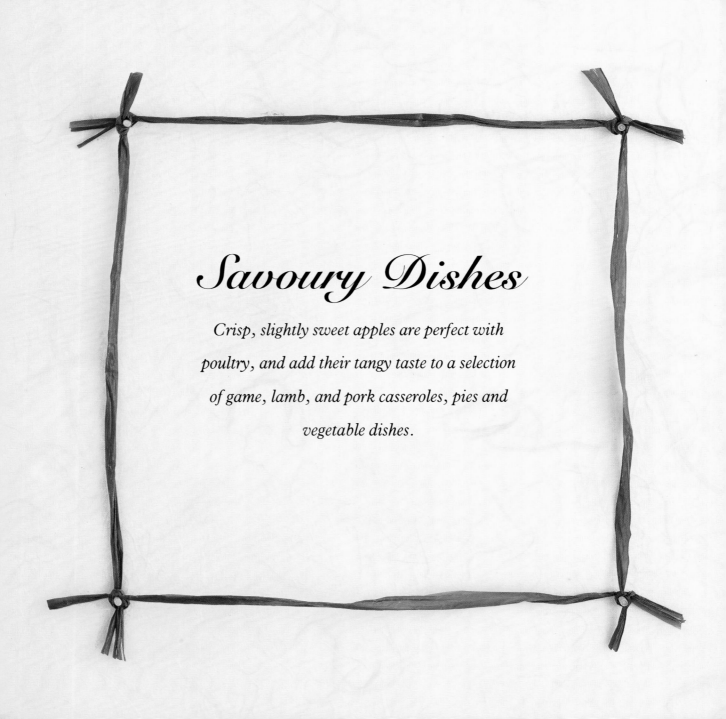

Savoury Dishes

Crisp, slightly sweet apples are perfect with poultry, and add their tangy taste to a selection of game, lamb, and pork casseroles, pies and vegetable dishes.

SOMERSET PORK WITH APPLES

A rich country dish using fresh apples and cider.

Serves 4

25g/1oz/2 tbsp butter

500g/1¼lb pork loin, cut into bite-size
pieces

12 baby onions, peeled

10ml/2 tsp grated lemon rind

300ml/½ pint/1¼ cups dry cider

150ml/¼ pint/²⁄₃ cup veal stock

2 eating apples, cored and sliced

45ml/3 tbsp chopped fresh parsley

100ml/3½fl oz/scant ½ cup
whipping cream

salt and ground black pepper

COOK'S TIP

It is advisable to remove the rind
from the pork before cutting into
pieces. This is best done with
sharp scissors or a sharp knife.

Heat the butter in a large heavy-based frying pan and sauté the pork in batches until brown. Transfer the pork to a bowl.

Add the onions to the pan, brown lightly, then stir in the lemon rind, cider and stock and boil for about 3 minutes. Return all the pork to the pan and cook gently for about 25 minutes until the pork is tender.

Stir the apples into the pan and cook for a further 5 minutes. Using a slotted spoon, transfer the pork, onions and apples to a warmed serving dish, cover and keep warm. Add the parsley and stir the cream into the pan and allow to bubble to thicken the sauce slightly. Season, then pour over the pork and serve immediately.

PORK AND APPLE HOT-POT

An economical and tasty dish using a cheaper cut of pork.

Serves 4

500g/1¼lb sparerib pork chops

30ml/2 tbsp sunflower oil

1 large onion, sliced

3 celery sticks, chopped

15ml/1 tbsp chopped fresh sage, or
   5ml/1 tsp dried

15ml/1 tbsp chopped fresh parsley

2 eating apples, peeled, cored and cut
   into thick wedges

150ml/¼ pint/⅔ cup apple juice

150ml/¼ pint/⅔ cup lamb, beef or
   vegetable stock

15ml/1 tbsp cornflour

450g/1lb par-boiled, peeled and
   sliced potatoes

melted butter, to glaze

salt and ground black pepper

sage leaves, to garnish

Remove any bones from the pork and cut the meat into even-size cubes. Sprinkle with seasoning.

Heat the oil in a pan and fry the onion and celery until golden. Remove and place half in the base of a casserole. Arrange the meat on top and sprinkle with half the herbs.

Add the apples and the rest of the onion, celery and herbs. Season to taste. Blend the apple juice with the stock and cornflour and pour over.

Preheat the oven to 190°C/375°F/Gas 5. Top with the sliced potatoes and brush with melted butter. Cover and cook in the oven for 50–60 minutes, removing the lid for the last 15 minutes to brown the potatoes. Serve immediately, garnished with sage leaves.

LAMB, LEEK AND APPLE PIE

An innovative combination where lamb and leeks are spiced up with apple.

Serves 4

675g/1½lb lamb neck fillets, cut into
  12 pieces
115g/4oz gammon, diced
1 onion, thinly sliced
350g/12oz leeks, sliced
1 large cooking apple (about 225g/
  8oz), peeled, cored and sliced
1.5–2.5ml/¼–½ tsp ground allspice
1.5–2.5ml/¼–½ tsp grated nutmeg
150ml/¼ pint/⅔ cup lamb, beef or
  vegetable stock
225g/8oz ready-made shortcrust pastry
beaten egg or milk, to glaze
salt and ground black pepper

COOK'S TIP
*When you are buying leeks, look
for those that are straight and
well-shaped. Avoid any that
have yellow, discoloured and
slimy leaves.*

Preheat the oven to 200°C/400°F/Gas 6. Layer the meats, onion, leeks and apple in a 900ml/1½ pint/3¾ cup pie dish, sprinkling in the spices and seasoning as you go. Pour in the stock.

On a lightly floured surface, roll out the pastry 2cm/¾in larger than the top of the pie dish. Cut a narrow strip from around the pastry, fit it around the dampened rim of the dish, then brush with water.

Lay the pastry over the filling and press the edges together to seal them. Brush the top with beaten egg or milk, and make a hole in the centre.

Bake the pie for 20 minutes, then reduce the oven temperature to 180°C/350°F/Gas 4 and continue to bake for 1–1¼ hours, covering the pie with foil if the pastry begins to become too brown. Serve immediately.

GUINEA FOWL WITH CIDER AND APPLES

Guinea fowl are farmed, so they are available quite frequently in supermarkets, usually fresh. Their flavour is reminiscent of an old-fashioned chicken – not really gamey, but they do have slightly darker meat.

Serves 4

1.75kg/4–4½lb guinea fowl

1 onion, halved

3 celery sticks

3 bay leaves

a little butter

300ml/½ pint/1¼ cups dry cider

150ml/¼ pint/⅔ cup chicken stock

2 small cooking apples (about 450g/
1lb), peeled and sliced

60ml/4 tbsp thick double cream

a few sage leaves, plus extra to garnish

30ml/2 tbsp chopped fresh parsley

salt and ground black pepper

If the guinea fowl is packed with its giblets, put them in a pan with water to cover, add half the onion, a stick of celery, a bay leaf and seasoning. Bring to the boil and simmer for about 30 minutes, or until you have about 150ml/¼ pint/⅔ cup of well-flavoured stock. Use this in the recipe instead of the chicken stock.

Preheat the oven to 190°C/375°F/Gas 5. Wash and wipe dry the bird and place the remaining onion half and a knob of butter inside the body cavity. Place the guinea fowl in a roasting dish, sprinkle with seasoning and dot with a few knobs of butter.

Pour the cider and chicken or home-made stock into the dish and cover with a lid or foil. Bake in the oven for 25 minutes per 450g/1lb, basting the bird occasionally.

Uncover for the last 20 minutes and baste well again. Slice the remaining celery and add it together with the prepared apples. When the guinea fowl is cooked, transfer it to a warm serving dish and keep warm. Remove the apples and celery with a slotted spoon and set aside.

Boil the liquid rapidly to reduce to about 150ml/¼ pint/⅔ cup. Stir in the cream, seasoning and the sage leaves, and cook for a few minutes more to reduce slightly. Return the apples to this pan with the parsley and warm through. Serve with or around the bird, garnished with sage leaves.

BRAISED RED CABBAGE WITH APPLES

The combination of red wine vinegar and sugar gives this dish a sweet, yet tart flavour. In France it is often served with game, but it is also delicious with pork, duck or cold sliced meats.

Serves 6–8

30ml/2 tbsp vegetable oil

2 onions, thinly sliced

2 eating apples, peeled, cored and thinly sliced

1 red cabbage (about 900g–1.2kg/ 2–2¹/₂lb), trimmed, cored, halved and thinly sliced

60ml/4 tbsp red wine vinegar

about 30ml/2 tbsp sugar

1.5ml/¹/₄ tsp ground cloves

5–10ml/1–2 tsp mustard seeds

50g/2oz/¹/₃ cup raisins or currants

about 120ml/4fl oz/¹/₂ cup red wine or water

15–30ml/1–2 tbsp redcurrant jelly (optional)

salt and ground black pepper

Heat the oil in a large heavy-based pan or flameproof casserole and cook the onions over medium heat until golden. Stir in the apples and cook, stirring, for a further 2–3 minutes until they are just softened.

Add the cabbage, red wine vinegar, sugar, cloves, mustard seeds, raisins or currants, red wine or water and seasoning. Stir until well mixed. Bring to the boil over a medium-high heat, stirring occasionally.

Cover and cook over a medium-low heat for about 35–40 minutes until the cabbage is tender and the liquid is just absorbed, stirring occasionally. Add a little more red wine or water if the pan boils dry before the cabbage is tender. Just before serving, stir in the redcurrant jelly, if using, to sweeten and glaze the cabbage.

Sweet Pastries and Cakes

Sharp, flavourful apples make a perfect contrast to light, crisp pastry in classic pies and tarts, and when combined with other fruits, make a tangy addition to a selection of deliciously moist cakes.

STRAWBERRY AND APPLE TART

A dish for lovers – apples and strawberries in perfect harmony.

Serves 4–6

*2 tart Bramley cooking apples (about
   450g/1lb), peeled, cored and sliced*
*200g/7oz/1¾ cups strawberries,
   halved*
60ml/4 tbsp sugar
15ml/1 tbsp cornflour

For the pastry
150g/5oz/1¼ cups self-raising flour
50g/2oz/⅔ cup rolled oats
50g/2oz/4 tbsp margarine

COOK'S TIP

*It is best to prepare apples just
before you use them. If you do
prepare them ahead, place the
cut pieces in a bowl of lemony
cold water to prevent them from
turning brown.*

Preheat the oven to 200°C/400°F/Gas 6. For the pastry, mix the flour and oats in a bowl and rub in the margarine evenly. Stir in cold water to bind and form a ball. Knead lightly until smooth. On a lightly floured surface, roll out the pastry and line a lightly greased 23cm/9in loose-based flan tin. Trim the edges, prick the base, line the pastry with greaseproof paper and fill with baking beans. Roll out the trimmings and make heart shapes with a cutter. Bake for 10 minutes, remove the paper and beans, and bake for 10–15 minutes until golden brown. Bake the hearts until golden. Place the apples in a pan with the strawberries, sugar and cornflour. Cover and cook gently, stirring, until the fruit is just tender. Spoon into the pastry case and decorate with the pastry hearts.

31

APPLE PIE

A comforting dish that will take you back to your childhood.

Serves 8

4 tart Granny Smith apples (about
  900g/2lb), sliced
15ml/1 tbsp fresh lemon juice
15ml/1 tbsp vanilla essence
115g/4oz/1/2 cup sugar
2.5ml/1/2 tsp ground cinnamon
20g/3/4oz/11/2 tbsp butter or margarine
1 egg yolk
10ml/2 tsp whipping cream

For the pastry
225g/8oz/2 cups self-raising flour
5ml/1 tsp salt
175g/6oz/3/4 cup lard
60–75ml/4–5 tbsp water
15ml/1 tbsp quick-cook tapioca

Preheat the oven to 230°C/450°F/Gas 8. To make the pastry, sift the flour and salt into a bowl. Rub in the lard until the mixture forms soft crumbs. Add the water, a tablespoon at a time, and form into a ball.

Cut the dough in half and shape each half into another ball. On a lightly floured surface, roll out one of the balls of pastry to a circle about 30cm/12in in diameter.

Line a lightly greased 23cm/9in loose-based flan tin, easing the dough in and being careful not to stretch it. Trim the edges carefully and keep the excess pastry for later. Sprinkle the quick-cook tapioca evenly over the base of the pastry case.

Roll out the remaining pastry to 3mm/1/8in thick and cut out eight large leaf shapes with a sharp knife. Cut the trimmings into enough smaller leaves to decorate the edges of the pie. Score the leaves with the back of a knife to make the leaf veins.

To make the filling, mix together the apples, lemon juice, vanilla essence, sugar and cinnamon. Tip into the pastry case and add dots of butter or margarine over the apple mixture.

Arrange the large pastry leaves in a decorative pattern on top, and decorate the edge with the smaller leaves. Mix the egg yolk with the cream and brush it over the leaves.

Bake in the preheated oven for 10 minutes. Reduce the oven temperature to 180°C/350°F/Gas 4. Cook for a further 35–45 minutes until the pastry is golden brown. Allow the pie to cool in the tin slightly before removing it and putting it on a wire cooling rack.

TARTE TATIN

This delicious caramelized fruit tart from France was originally created by the Tatin sisters who ran a
popular restaurant in Sologne in the Orléanais.

Serves 4
75g/3oz/6 tbsp butter, softened
90ml/6 tbsp soft light brown sugar
10 Cox's Pippin, peeled, cored and
*   thickly sliced*
whipped cream, to serve (optional)

For the pastry
50g/2oz/4 tbsp butter, softened
45ml/3 tbsp caster sugar
1 egg
115g/4oz/1 cup plain flour
pinch of salt

COOK'S TIP
Cox's Pippins apples are perfect
for this tart because they hold
their shape so well. If they are
not available, use another firm,
sweet eating apple instead.

To make the pastry, cream the butter and sugar in a bowl until pale and creamy. Beat in the egg, then sift in the flour and salt and mix to a soft dough. On a lightly floured surface, knead gently and bring the dough together into a ball.

Grease a 23cm/9in cake tin, then add 50g/2oz/4 tbsp of the butter. Place the cake tin on the hob and melt the butter gently. Remove from the heat and sprinkle over 60ml/4 tbsp of the sugar.

Arrange the apple slices on top, then sprinkle with the remaining sugar and dot with the remaining butter.

Preheat the oven to 230°C/450°F/Gas 8. Place the cake tin on the hob again over a low to moderate heat for about 15 minutes, until a light golden caramel forms on the base. Remove the tin from the heat.

Roll out the pastry on a lightly floured surface to a round the same size as the tin and lay on top of the apples. Tuck the pastry edges down round the sides of the apples. Trim away any excess pastry.

Bake for about 20–25 minutes, until the pastry is golden brown. Remove the tart from the oven and leave to stand for about 5 minutes.

Place an upturned plate on top of the tin and, holding the two together with a dish towel, turn the apple tart out on to the plate. Serve while still warm with whipped cream, if wished.

DUTCH APPLE TART

Flaked almonds give this tart a wonderful crunchiness.

Serves 4–6

6 eating apples, peeled, cored
  and grated
60ml/4 tbsp soft light brown sugar
1.5ml/¼ tsp vanilla essence
2.5ml/¼ tsp ground cinnamon
25g/1oz/scant ¼ cup raisins
25g/1oz/¼ cup flaked almonds, toasted
15ml/1 tbsp caster sugar, for dredging
whipped cream, to serve

For the pastry
175g/6oz/1½ cups plain flour
130g/4½oz/generous ½ cup butter,
  cubed and softened
90ml/6 tbsp caster sugar
pinch of salt

Preheat the oven to 180°C/350°F/Gas 4. Lightly butter a 20cm/8in round springform tin and dust with a little plain flour.

To make the pastry, place the flour in a mixing bowl with the butter and sugar, then squeeze together to form a firm dough. Knead the pastry lightly and bring it together into a ball. Chill, covered or wrapped, for 1 hour.

Roll two-thirds of the chilled pastry out on a lightly floured surface to form a 25cm/10in round. Use this to line the base and two-thirds up the sides of the prepared tin, pressing the pastry up the sides with your fingers. Trim away any excess pastry.

Mix together the apples, sugar, vanilla essence, cinnamon, raisins and almonds in a bowl. Spoon into the lined tin and level the surface. Fold the pastry edge above the level of the apples down over the filling.

Roll out the remaining pastry and cut into eight 1cm/½in strips. Brush the strips with cold water and sprinkle over the caster sugar. Lay the strips on top of the tart in a lattice pattern, securing the ends to the folded-over edge with a little water.

Bake in the centre of the oven for 1 hour, or until the pastry is golden brown. Remove and leave to cool in the tin. When the tart is cold, carefully remove it from the tin. Serve cut into slices with whipped cream.

APPLE MERINGUE TART

Like pears, quinces substitute well in most apple recipes and are quite delicious. If you ever find any quinces, this is the ideal tart to use them in.

Serves 6

675g/1½lb eating apples
juice of ½ lemon
25g/1oz/2 tbsp butter
60ml/4 tbsp demerara sugar
cream, to serve (optional)

For the pastry
50g/2oz/½ cup plain flour
75g/3oz/¾ cup wholemeal flour
pinch of salt
115g/4oz/½ cup caster sugar
75g/3oz/6 tbsp butter
1 egg, separated, plus 1 egg white

To make the pastry, sift the flours into a bowl with the salt, adding in the wheat flakes from the sieve. Add 15ml/1 tbsp of the caster sugar and rub in the butter until the mixture forms soft crumbs.

Work in the egg yolk and, if necessary, 15–30ml/1–2 tbsp cold water. Knead lightly and bring together into a ball. Chill, covered or wrapped, for between 10 and 20 minutes.

Preheat the oven to 190°C/375°F/Gas 5. Roll the chilled pastry out on a lightly floured surface to form a 23cm/9in round and use to line a 20cm/8in flan tin. Line with greaseproof paper and fill with baking beans. Bake blind for 15 minutes, then remove the paper and beans and cook for a further 5–10 minutes, until the pastry is crisp.

Meanwhile, peel, core and slice the apples, then toss in lemon juice. Melt the butter, add the demerara sugar and fry the apple until golden and just tender. Arrange in the pastry case.

Preheat the oven to 220°C/425°F/Gas 7. Whisk the egg white until it is stiff. Whisk in half the remaining caster sugar, then carefully fold in the rest. Pipe the meringue over the apples. Bake for 6–7 minutes. Serve the tart hot or cold, with cream if wished.

APPLE AND PEAR FRYING PAN CAKE

This unusual cake, lightly spiced with cinnamon and nutmeg and baked in a frying pan, is impressively simple to make. It is delicious served hot.

Serves 6

1 cooking apple (about 225g/8oz),
  peeled, cored and thinly sliced
1 pear, peeled, cored and thinly sliced
50g/2oz/½ cup chopped walnuts
5ml/1 tsp ground cinnamon
5ml/1 tsp grated nutmeg
3 eggs
75g/3oz/¾ cup plain flour
30ml/2 tbsp light brown sugar
175ml/6fl oz/¾ cup milk
5ml/1 tsp vanilla essence
50g/2 oz/4 tbsp butter or margarine
icing sugar, for sprinkling
cream or ice cream, to serve (optional)

Preheat the oven to 190°C/375°F/Gas 5. In a large bowl, toss together the apple and pear slices, walnuts, cinnamon and nutmeg until thoroughly combined. Set aside.

With an electric mixer, beat together the eggs, plain flour, light brown sugar, milk and vanilla essence. Melt the butter or margarine in a 23–25cm/9–10in ovenproof frying pan over moderate heat. Add the apple mixture and cook for about 5 minutes, until it is lightly caramelized, stirring occasionally. When cooked, make sure that the apple and pear mixture is evenly distributed in the frying pan.

Pour the sponge mixture over the fruit and nuts. Transfer the frying pan to the preheated oven and bake for about 30 minutes until the cake is puffy and pulling away from the sides of the pan. Serve hot sprinkled lightly with icing sugar, with cream or ice cream as an accompaniment, if you wish.

COOK'S TIP
This cake should be served straight from the frying pan. There is no need to transfer it to a serving plate first.

CRANBERRY AND APPLE RING

Tangy cranberries add an unusual flavour to this light-textured cake. It is best eaten very fresh.

Serves 4–6

225g/8oz/2 cups self-raising flour

5ml/1 tsp ground cinnamon

90ml/6 tbsp light muscovado sugar

1 crisp eating apple, cored and diced

*75g/3oz/²⁄₃ cup fresh or frozen
  cranberries*

60ml/4 tbsp sunflower oil

150ml/³⁄₄ pint/²⁄₃ cup apple juice

*cranberry jelly and apple slices,
  to decorate*

Preheat the oven to 180°C/350°F/Gas 4. Lightly grease a 1 litre/1¼ pint/ 4 cup ring tin with oil. It is easiest to do this with a pastry brush, or you could use a piece of kitchen paper.

Sift together the flour and ground cinnamon, then stir in the sugar. Toss together the diced apple and cranberries. Stir the fruit into the dry ingredients, then add the sunflower oil and apple juice and beat well until thoroughly combined.

Spoon the cake mixture into the prepared ring tin and bake in the preheated oven for about 35–40 minutes, or until the cake is firm to the touch. Turn the cake out and leave it to cool on a wire cooling rack.

Just before serving, warm the cranberry jelly in a small saucepan over a gentle heat. Decorate the top of the ring with the prepared apple slices, then drizzle the warmed cranberry jelly over the apple pieces, letting it run down the sides of the ring.

COOK'S TIP

Fresh cranberries are now readily available throughout the winter months and if you don't use them all at once, they can be frozen for up to a year.

APPLE CRUMBLE CAKE

A rich and filling cake which is excellent served with thick cream or custard.

Serves 8–10

For the topping

75g/3oz/³⁄4 cup self-raising flour

2.5ml/¹⁄2 tsp ground cinnamon

40g/1¹⁄2oz/3 tbsp butter

30ml/2 tbsp caster sugar

For the base

50g/2oz/4 tbsp butter, softened

90ml/6 tbsp caster sugar

1 egg, beaten

115g/4oz/1 cup self-raising
flour, sifted

2 cooking apples (about 450g/1lb),
peeled, cored and sliced

50g/2oz/¹⁄3 cup sultanas

To decorate

1 red eating apple, cored, thinly sliced
and tossed in lemon juice

30ml/2 tbsp caster sugar, sifted

pinch of ground cinnamon

Preheat the oven to 180°C/350°F/Gas 4. Lightly grease and line a deep 18cm/7in springform tin.

To make the topping, sift the flour and cinnamon together into a bowl. Rub in the butter until the mixture forms soft crumbs, then stir in the sugar. Set aside until needed.

To make the base for the cake, put the butter, sugar, egg and flour into a bowl and beat for 1–2 minutes until smooth. Spoon into the prepared tin and even out the surface.

Mix together the apple slices and sultanas and spread them evenly over the top of the base. Sprinkle with the topping.

Bake in the centre of the preheated oven for about 1 hour. Then remove from the oven and cool in the tin for 10 minutes before turning out on to a wire cooling rack and peeling off the lining paper. Serve warm or cool, decorated with the prepared slices of red eating apple and with caster sugar and cinnamon sprinkled over the top.

Hot Puddings

Apples make a perfect addition to warming desserts,

delicate sponges and hearty, satisfying crumbles;

or try them caramelized in a deliciously sweet and

sticky toffee-flavoured pudding.

CARAMELIZED APPLES

A sweet, sticky dessert which is very quickly made, and usually very quickly eaten!

Serves 4

675g/1½lb eating apples
115g/4oz/½ cup unsalted butter
25g/1oz/7 tbsp fresh white
   breadcrumbs
50g/2oz/½ cup ground almonds
finely grated rind of 2 lemons
60ml/4 tbsp golden syrup
60ml/4 tbsp clotted cream, to serve

COOK'S TIP
The easiest and quickest way to make breadcrumbs is to put slices of bread into a food processor or blender. Roughly chop the bread for several seconds until breadcrumbs form. Take care not to overchop.

Peel and core the apples. Cut them into 1cm/½in thick rings. Heat a wok and add the butter. When the butter has melted, add the apple rings and stir-fry for 4 minutes until golden and tender. Remove from the wok, reserving the butter. Add the breadcrumbs to the hot butter and stir-fry for 1 minute.

Stir in the ground almonds and lemon rind and stir-fry for a further 3 minutes, stirring constantly. Sprinkle the breadcrumb mix over the apples, then drizzle warmed golden syrup over the top. Serve with the cream.

EVE'S PUDDING

This pudding is irresistible! The tempting, tender apples beneath the rich sponge topping are the reason for its name.

Serves 4–6

115g/4oz/½ cup butter
115g/4oz/½ cup caster sugar
2 eggs, beaten
grated rind and juice of 1 lemon
90g/3½oz/scant 1 cup self-raising flour
40g/1½oz/⅓ cup ground almonds
115g/4oz/scant ½ cup soft brown sugar
3 cooking apples (about 675g/1½lb),
  cored and thinly sliced
25g/1oz/¼ cup flaked almonds
whipped cream, to serve

Beat together the butter and caster sugar in a large bowl until the mixture is very light and fluffy.

Gradually beat the eggs into the butter mixture, beating well after each addition, then fold in the lemon rind, flour and ground almonds.

Mix together the brown sugar, apples and lemon juice, tip into the dish and level out. Add the sponge mixture, then the almonds. Bake for 40–45 minutes, until golden. Serve warm with whipped cream.

CHUNKY APPLE BAKE

This filling, economical family pudding is a good way to use up slightly stale bread – any type of bread will do, but wholemeal is richest in fibre.

Serves 4

2 cooking apples (about 450g/1lb)

*75g/3oz wholemeal bread,
   without crusts*

115g/4oz/½ cup cottage cheese

*45ml/3 tbsp light muscovado
   sugar*

*200ml/7fl oz/⅞ cup semi-skimmed
   milk*

5ml/1 tsp demerara sugar

COOK'S TIP

You may need to adjust the amount of milk used, depending on the dryness of the bread; the staler the bread, the more milk it will absorb.

Preheat the oven to 220°C/425°F/Gas 7. Peel the apples, cut them in quarters and remove the cores.

Roughly chop the apples into even-size pieces, about 1cm/½in across. Cut the bread into 1cm/½in dice.

Toss together the apples, bread, cottage cheese and muscovado sugar. Stir in the milk and then tip the mixture into a wide ovenproof dish. Sprinkle with the demerara sugar.

Bake for 30–35 minutes, or until golden brown and bubbling. Serve hot.

APPLE AND KUMQUAT SPONGE PUDDINGS

The kumquats provide a surprising tanginess in this pudding.

Serves 8

*150g/5oz/generous ½ cup butter, at
   room temperature*
*175g/6oz cooking apples, peeled and
   thinly sliced*
75g/3oz kumquats, thinly sliced
*150g/5oz/generous ½ cup golden
   caster sugar*
2 eggs
115g/4oz/1 cup self-raising flour

For the sauce

75g/3oz kumquats, thinly sliced
90ml/6 tbsp caster sugar
250ml/8fl oz/1 cup water
150ml/¼ pint/⅔ cup crème fraîche
*5ml/1 tsp cornflour mixed with 10ml/
   2 tsp water*
lemon juice, to taste

Prepare the steamer. Lightly butter eight 150ml/¼ pint/⅔ cup dariole moulds or ramekins and put a disc of buttered greaseproof paper on the base of each one.

Melt 25g/1oz/2 tbsp butter in a frying pan. Add the apples, kumquats and 30ml/2 tbsp sugar and cook over a moderate heat for 5–8 minutes or until the apples start to soften and the sugar begins to caramelize. Remove from the heat and leave to cool.

Meanwhile, cream the remaining butter with the remaining sugar until the mixture is pale and fluffy. Add the eggs, one at a time, beating well after each addition. Fold in the flour.

Divide the apple and kumquat mixture among the prepared moulds. Top with the sponge mixture. Cover the moulds and put them into the steamer. Steam on top of the stove for 45 minutes.

To make the sauce, put the kumquats, sugar and water in a frying pan and bring to the boil, stirring to dissolve the sugar. Simmer for 5 minutes. Stir in the crème fraîche and bring back to the boil, stirring.

Remove from the heat and whisk in the cornflour mixture. Return the pan to the heat and simmer gently for a further 2 minutes, stirring. Add lemon juice to taste. Turn out the puddings and serve hot with the sauce.

APPLE COUSCOUS PUDDING

This unusual couscous mixture makes a delicious pudding with a rich fruity flavour, but virtually no fat.

Serves 4

600ml/1 pint/2¹/₂ cups apple juice
115g/4oz/²/₃ cup couscous
40g/1¹/₂oz/¹/₄ cup sultanas
2.5ml/¹/₂ tsp mixed spice
1 large Bramley cooking apple (about
*   225g/8oz), peeled, cored and sliced*
30ml/2 tbsp demerara sugar
natural low-fat yogurt, to serve

Preheat the oven to 200°C/400°F/Gas 6. Place the apple juice, couscous, sultanas and spice in a pan and bring to the boil, stirring. Cover and simmer for 10–12 minutes, until all the free liquid is absorbed.

Spoon half the couscous mixture into a 1.2 litre/2 pint/5 cup ovenproof dish and top with half the apple slices. Top with the remaining couscous.

Arrange the remaining apple slices overlapping over the top and sprinkle with demerara sugar. Bake in the oven for 25–30 minutes, or until golden brown. Serve hot with yogurt.

COOK'S TIP
To ring the changes, substitute
other dried fruits for the sultanas
in this recipe – try chopped dates
or ready-to-eat pears, figs,
peaches or apricots.

APPLE AND BLACKBERRY NUT CRUMBLE

This much-loved dish is perhaps one of the simplest and most delicious of hot British puddings.

Serves 4

4 Bramley cooking apples (about 900g/
*   2lb), peeled, cored and sliced*
115g/4oz/½ cup butter, cubed
115g/4oz/generous ½ cup soft light
*   brown sugar*
175g/6oz/1¾ cups blackberries

For the topping
75g/3oz/¼ cup wholemeal flour
75g/3oz/¼ cup plain flour
2.5ml/½ tsp ground cinnamon
45ml/3 tbsp chopped mixed
*   nuts, toasted*
custard, cream or ice cream, to serve

Preheat the oven to 180°C/350°F/Gas 4. Lightly butter a 1.2 litre/2 pint/ 5 cup ovenproof dish.

Place the apples in a pan with 25g/1oz/2 tbsp of the butter, 30ml/2 tbsp of the sugar and 15ml/1 tbsp water. Cover and cook gently for 10 minutes, until just tender. Remove from the heat and gently stir in the blackberries. Spoon the mixture into the dish and set aside.

To make the topping, sift the flours and cinnamon into a bowl (tip in any wheat flakes left in the sieve). Add the remaining butter and rub into the flour with your fingertips until the mixture resembles fine breadcrumbs.

Stir in the remaining 90ml/6 tbsp sugar and the nuts and mix well. Sprinkle the crumble topping over the fruit. Bake for 35–40 minutes, until the top is golden brown. Serve hot with custard, cream or ice cream.

APPLE CHARLOTTE

This classic dessert takes its name from the straight-sided tin with heart-shaped handles in which it is baked. The buttery bread crust encases a thick sweet, yet sharp apple purée.

Serves 6

5 cooking apples (about 1.2kg/2½lb)
30ml/2 tbsp water
115g/4oz/generous ½ cup soft light
* brown sugar*
2.5ml/½ tsp ground cinnamon
1.5ml/¼ tsp grated nutmeg
7 slices firm-textured sliced white bread
65–75g/2½–3oz/5–6 tbsp butter,
* melted*
custard, to serve (optional)

> COOK'S TIP
> *If preferred, microwave the apples without water in a large glass dish at High (100% power), tightly covered, for 15 minutes. Add the sugar and spices and microwave, uncovered, for about 15 minutes more until very thick, stirring once or twice.*

Peel, quarter and core the apples. Cut into thick slices and put in a large heavy-based pan with the water. Cook, covered, over a moderate heat for 5 minutes, and then uncover the pan and cook for 10 minutes until the apples are very soft. Add the sugar, cinnamon and nutmeg and continue cooking for 5–10 minutes, stirring frequently, until the apples are soft and thick. (There should be about 750ml/1¼ pints/3 cups of apple purée.)

Preheat the oven to 200°C/400°F/Gas 6. Trim the crusts from the bread and brush with melted butter on one side. Cut two slices into triangles and use as many as necessary to cover the base of a 1.4 litre/2¼ pint/6 cup charlotte tin or soufflé dish, placing them buttered-side down and fitting them tightly. Cut fingers of bread the same height as the tin or dish and use them to line the sides completely, overlapping them slightly and making sure there are no gaps.

Pour the apple purée into the tin or dish. Cover the top with bread slices, buttered-side up, cutting them as necessary to fit.

Bake the charlotte for 20 minutes. Reduce the oven temperature to 180°C/350°F/Gas 4 and bake for a further 25 minutes until golden brown and firm. Leave to stand for 15 minutes. To turn out, place a serving plate over the tin or dish, hold tightly, and invert, then lift off the tin or dish. Serve hot with custard, if wished.

BAKED APPLES WITH CARAMEL SAUCE

The creamy caramel sauce adds a touch of sophistication to this traditional dish.

Serves 6

3 Granny Smith apples, cored but
not peeled

3 Red Delicious apples, cored but
not peeled

150g/5oz/3/4 cup soft brown sugar

175ml/6fl oz/3/4 cup water

2.5ml/1/2 tsp grated nutmeg

1.5ml/1/4 tsp ground
black pepper

40g/11/2oz/1/4 cup walnut pieces

40g/11/2oz/1/4 cup sultanas

50g/2oz/4 tbsp butter or
margarine, diced

For the caramel sauce

15g/1/2 oz/1 tbsp butter or margarine

120ml/4fl oz/1/2 cup whipping cream

> **COOK'S TIP**
> *Use a mixture of firm red and*
> *gold pears instead of the apples.*
> *Cook for 10 minutes longer.*

Preheat the oven to 190°C/375°F/Gas 5. Lightly grease a baking tin. With a small knife, enlarge the core opening at the stem end of each apple to about 2.5cm/1in in diameter. Arrange the apples in the tin, stem-end up.

In a small pan, combine the brown sugar, water, nutmeg and pepper. Boil the mixture, stirring, for 6 minutes. Mix together the walnuts and sultanas. Spoon some of the walnut mixture into each apple. Top with some diced butter or margarine. Spoon the sugar sauce over and around the apples. Bake, basting occasionally, until the apples are just tender, about 50 minutes. Put the apples in a serving dish, reserving the sauce in the baking dish. Keep the apples warm.

To make the caramel sauce, mix the butter or margarine, cream and reserved sauce in a pan. Bring to the boil, stirring, and simmer for 2 minutes until thickened. Let the sauce cool slightly before serving.

APPLE SOUFFLE OMELETTE

Apples sautéed until they are slightly caramelized make a delicious autumn filling for omelettes.

Serves 2

4 eggs, separated
30ml/2 tbsp single cream
15ml/1 tbsp caster sugar
15g/¹/₂oz/1 tbsp butter
icing sugar, for dredging

For the filling
25g/1oz/2 tbsp butter
30ml/2 tbsp soft light brown sugar
1 eating apple, peeled, cored and sliced
45ml/3 tbsp single cream

To make the filling, heat the butter and sugar in a frying pan and sauté the apple slices until just tender. Stir in the cream and keep warm.

Place the egg yolks in a bowl with the cream and sugar and beat well. Whisk the egg whites until stiff, then fold into the yolk mixture.

Melt the butter in a large heavy-based frying pan, pour in the soufflé mixture and spread evenly. Cook for 1 minute until golden underneath, then place under a hot grill to brown the top.

Slide the omelette on to a plate, add the apple mixture, then fold over. Sift the icing sugar over thickly, then mark in a criss-cross pattern with a hot metal skewer. Serve immediately.

Cold Desserts

For a special occasion meal, tart, fresh apples make a
fabulous finale when combined with roasted hazelnuts
in a crisp, layered shortcake, and with blackberries
in two spectacular iced desserts.

BLACKBERRY AND APPLE ROMANOFF

Rich yet fruity, this dessert is popular with most people and very quick to make.

Serves 6–8

*3–4 sharp eating apples, peeled, cored
  and chopped*

45ml/3 tbsp caster sugar

250ml/8fl oz/1 cup whipping cream

5ml/1 tsp grated lemon rind

90ml/6 tbsp Greek-style yogurt

*4–6 crisp meringues (about 50g/2oz),
  roughly crumbled*

*225g/8oz/2 cups fresh or
  frozen blackberries*

*whipped cream, a few blackberries and
  mint leaves, to decorate*

COOK'S TIP

*You can also make this into a
delicious ice cream, though the
texture of the frozen berries
makes it difficult to scoop if it is
frozen for more than 4–6 hours.*

With clear film, line a 900ml/1½ pint/3¾ cup pudding basin. Toss the apples into a pan with 30ml/2 tbsp sugar and cook for 2–3 minutes, or until softening. Mash with a fork and leave to cool.

Whip the cream and fold in the lemon rind, yogurt, the remaining sugar, the apples and the crumbled meringues.

Gently stir in the blackberries, then tip the mixture into the pudding basin and freeze for 1–3 hours.

Turn out on to a plate and remove the clear film. Serve decorated with piped cream, blackberries and mint leaves.

APPLE AND HAZELNUT SHORTCAKE

This variation of a traditional recipe will be popular with all the family.

Serves 8–10

150g/5oz/1¼ cups wholemeal flour

50g/2oz/½ cup ground hazelnuts

90ml/6 tbsp icing sugar, sifted

150g/5oz/generous ½ cup unsalted
*   butter or margarine*

3 sharp eating apples

5ml/1 tsp lemon juice

15–30ml/1–2 tbsp caster sugar, or to
*   taste*

15ml/1 tbsp chopped fresh mint, or
*   5ml/1 tsp dried*

250ml/8fl oz/1 cup whipping cream or
*   crème fraîche*

few drops of vanilla essence

few mint sprigs and whole hazelnuts,
*   to decorate*

Process the flour, ground hazelnuts and icing sugar with the butter in a food processor or blender in short bursts, or rub the butter into the dry ingredients until they come together into a ball. (Don't overwork the mixture.) Add a very little iced water if necessary. Knead briefly, then chill, covered or wrapped, for about 30 minutes.

Preheat the oven to 160°C/325°F/Gas 3. Cut the chilled dough in half and roll out each half, on a lightly floured surface, to form an 18cm/7in round. Place on greaseproof paper on baking sheets and bake for about 40 minutes, or until crisp. If the shortcakes are browning too much, move them down in the oven to a lower shelf. Allow to cool.

Peel, core and chop the apples into a pan with the lemon juice. Add sugar to taste, then cook for about 2–3 minutes, until just softening. Mash the apple gently with the fresh mint or dried and leave to cool.

Whip the cream or crème fraîche with the vanilla essence. Place one shortcake base on a serving plate. Carefully spread half the apple and then half the cream or crème fraîche on top of the shortcake.

Place the second shortcake on top, then spread over the remaining apple and cream, swirling the top layer of cream gently. Serve immediately decorated with mint sprigs and a few whole hazelnuts.

FROZEN APPLE AND BLACKBERRY TERRINE

Apples and blackberries are a classic autumn combination; they really complement each other. This pretty, three-layered terrine can be frozen, so you can enjoy it at any time of year.

Serves 6

2 cooking or eating apples (about 450g/1lb)

300ml/½ pint/1¼ cups sweet cider

15ml/1 tbsp clear honey

5ml/1 tsp vanilla essence

200g/7oz/scant 2 cups fresh or frozen blackberries, thawed

15ml/1 tbsp/1 sachet powdered gelatine

2 egg whites

fresh apple slices and blackberries, to decorate

COOK'S TIP

For a quicker version, set the mixture without layering. Purée the fruit, stir the dissolved gelatine and whisked egg whites into the mixture, turn into the tin and leave to set.

Peel, core and chop the apples and place them in a pan, with half the cider. Bring the cider to the boil, and then cover the pan and let the apples simmer gently until tender.

Tip the apples into a food processor or blender and process them to a smooth purée. Stir in the honey and vanilla. Add half the blackberries to half the apple purée, and then process again until smooth. Sieve the purée to remove the blackberry pips.

Heat the remaining cider until it is almost boiling, and then sprinkle the gelatine over and stir until the gelatine has completely dissolved. Add half the gelatine mixture to the apple purée and half to the blackberry purée.

Leave the purées to cool until almost set. Whisk the egg whites until they are stiff. Quickly fold them into the apple purée. Remove half the purée to another bowl. Stir the remaining whole blackberries into half the apple purée, and then tip this into a 1.75 litre/3 pint/7½ cup loaf tin.

Top with the blackberry purée and spread it evenly. Finally, add a layer of the apple purée and smooth it evenly. If necessary, freeze each layer until firm before adding the next.

Freeze until firm. To serve, allow to stand at room temperature for about 20 minutes to soften, and then cut in slices, decorated with the fresh apple slices and blackberries.

INDEX